The Durni Dozen

*How to use trust and
effective relationship-building
to create sales success*

by
Robin Arthur Durni

 FriesenPress

One Printers Way
Altona, MB R0G 0B0
Canada

www.friesenpress.com

ISBN
978-1-03-916845-9 (Hardcover)
978-1-03-916844-2 (Paperback)
978-1-03-916846-6 (eBook)

1. BUSINESS & ECONOMICS, SALES & SELLING

Distributed to the trade by The Ingram Book Company

In memory of

My beloved mother Patricia Jane Roberts-Durni
The most courageous person I have ever known.
1920 – 1968

My beloved son
Gavin Gullo Durni
My best friend and love of my life.
1984 – 2014

Table of Contents

Introduction:
The Beginning of
My Journey in Sales

You do not get a second chance to make a good first impression.

The year 1968 changed my life, as it did for many others. It also ulti-mately led me to my lifelong career in sales. You see, I had been working at the Bethlehem Steel Plant in Buffalo, New York. I'd started out in the Boiler Department at the bottom as Boiler Washer Helper (cleaning the inside of boilers during routine maintenance), and on a swing shift. My father and two of his brothers also worked at the plant. After a year, I got into a non-union division called the Fuel Department with the help of my Uncle Victor. This was a great opportunity and was also a day-shift position. Once again, I started at the bottom as a Chart Boy (every day changing charts on the hundreds of control devices that monitored and controlled heat and fuel air ratios for the entire plant). Having a day shift position, allowed me to get a second job at Jacobi Brothers selling clothes, and a third job clearing tables and stocking bar at night at a place called Grandview Casino. I kept busy.

My younger brother Keith and I were also taking care of our mother who was a disabled Polio victim from the 1948 epidemic. Mom was confined to a wheelchair and she was without a doubt, the most courageous person I have ever known.

Along came 1968. I was 23 in July and the draft was calling me because my younger brother was now also draftable. So I chose to join the United States Marine Corps. Off I went to Paris Island for my Recruit Training. Paris Island is a story in itself, as it certainly lives up to its reputation. Camp Lejeune was next for Advanced Infantry Training.

But when I came home on leave from training, on leave before I traveled to Vietnam, my beloved mother passed away. This was devastating for us all. After an extended leave for family loss, I had to continue on to San Diego for more training, and then on to Vietnam.

An Hoa, 60 miles inland from Da Nang, was my base of operation for the duration of my tour. I was assigned to learn the duties of a Forward Observer from the existing FO because he was rotating home. The next morning, after a harrowing first night, My FO and I went with a lead squad to patrol ahead of the company. Aside from being scared to death and having to learn a new skill set that everyone depended upon, one of our planes had a problem and its bombs hung up then dropped on our position. Most were lost. This was only a glimpse at what was to come.

I returned home, thankfully, at the end of my tour with the rank of Sergeant, a Meritorious Combat Promotion. I tried to go back to working the same three jobs, but my hearing was so damaged from combat that the doctors advised me to leave the Steel Plant and find other work. I had no idea then that this ending would be the beginning of an incredible journey.

By happy coincidence, I met a sales representative who sold for a medical device company. He said, "You have boundless energy. Why don't you get a job in sales?" I was just home from Vietnam and had no college degree. I didn't think I'd have a chance in a field like that. But the sales rep invited me to ride with him for a few days, so I did and I loved it.

The medical equipment sales industry was at the beginning of total joint technology while trauma devices were also at a point of new technology. We went into several hospitals and even went to the Emergency Room,

Operating Room, and Orthopedic Floor in each facility. While there, we viewed X-rays with surgeons, talked to nurses, and even visited a patient with a surgeon.

Having the opportunity to be so involved in a business was amazing. We worked with the medical staff to help the outcome of patients! I was hooked.

The compression hip screw, a hip fracture device that ended up being the gold standard, was known as a gadget. When I started in this business, a hip fracture was synonymous with death. Think about that. You broke a hip, and in many cases, it was a death sentence. Well, then you think about what they were using to fix hip fractures at that time. Fixed angle devices had sharp ends, and healing was a bit of a crap shoot.

Do people move if they're in pain? No. If it hurts, they don't want to move, so they stay in the bed. Next thing you know, they develop pulmonary issues, things never heal, and they pass away. Thankfully, we've evolved quite a bit since that time in the medical world. I told the sales rep that I really liked what he did, and he got me an interview with his boss.

His boss lived in Pittsburg and owned one of the original independent distributorships for the Northeast. I bought a suit, a new pair of shoes, a shirt and tie, and I flew down to Pittsburg on the ticket he sent. I got off the plane, and there he was, waiting for me, right at the exit gate.

He invited me to have a cup of coffee, and after what couldn't have been more than ten minutes, he pulled a ticket out of his pocket and said, "Why don't you get back on that plane to Buffalo?"

I said, "Well, sir, I guess I didn't do very well."

He said, "No, you did fine."

"But we didn't talk about sales."

"Robin, let me tell you something. An orthopedic surgeon makes up his mind whether he likes you in 60 seconds or less. You will do fine."

It's still true today. In fact, I think it's 30 seconds or less, or maybe even 15 seconds, because today's surgeons/customers are moving at an infinitely faster pace than they were in the early 1970s, when in fact there are many more sales representatives trying to get a portion of a surgeons' time.

Let's face it: Surgeons or other types of customers probably don't need you. They've got somebody providing everything they want. So it's even more important today to build trust through listening and showing them that you value them. In fact, it's fundamental.

I took the job offer, quit the steel plant, and moved to Albany, New York, early in the fall of 1972.

There was no real sales volume where I started, and I had a territory that went from Plattsburg, to Albany, to Poughkeepsie, all in eastern New York State. Much of that region is very rural, but that was my dirt. My first year in the business, my sales were $22,000. You can do the math at 15 percent commission.

Six months later, my new boss died in an accident on his farm. Management came in for the funeral. Afterwards, they offered all of his 20 plus sales representatives independent contractor distributorships. No doubt, I had not earned the right to be a distributor, but I took it. I signed the paper, and that's how I became a distributor. Ha! A distributor with a sales force of one, myself.

During my many years in this profession, I developed a deep understanding of the fundamentals of successful sales. I learned that you have at least a 50/50 chance of starting a new relationship during that first impression. I like the 50 percent chance on the positive side, or glass-half-full thinking. All you have to do is listen!

Recently, Harvard Business Review. [1](Harvard Business Review, https://hbr.org/2006/07/what-makes-a-good-salesman) did a study about salespeople. One of their findings was that a salesperson should have two qualities: empathy with customers—the ability to put themselves in someone else's shoes and understand their feelings—and the ability to overcome the customer's hesitation to buy. That's our job.

Empathy plays a huge role in the sales process.

Empathy: The ability to put ourselves in someone else's shoes and understand their feelings.

This is why my system for developing your skills as a salesperson begins with relationship building. If you can't build relationships, you can't sustain sales with a customer base. In order to support that relationship building and advance the product, this system has 12 steps. These 12 steps of the sales process as I developed them throughout my tenure are things that I used, and I still use, on a daily basis. Many of these steps can be applied to your personal lives and not just your business life. I call them the Durni Dozen:

1. Preparation
2. Research
3. Listening
4. Body language
5. Voice control
6. Use of props
7. Ownership
8. Product relevance
9. Creating value
10. Advancing the sale
11. Debriefing
12. Following-up

Let's get started to learn who you can become as a successful salesperson.

---

1   (Harvard Business Review, https://hbr.org/2006/07/what-makes-a-good-salesman)

The Foundation:
Relationship Building

Relationship building is the foundation of the Durni Dozen.

Please don't confuse relationship building with the relationship type of salespeople.

Let's tap into the importance of the customer and the potential to build a relationship with an exercise I call the Foundation.

When I teach the Durni Dozen in my Master Series, I write RELATIONSHIPS at the top of a flip chart. Just below that I write, EXISTING or NEW (this exercise refers to both). Next, I ask the class, "What is most important in building and maintaining relationships?" Then I extend an arrow down and perpendicular to that arrow, I write TRUST. "What is needed to build trust?" LISTENING. Then I ask, "Who is more important, you or the customer?" The customer is more important and they need to know that. Finally, I draw one more downward arrow and under it I write VALUE. Once the customer realizes that you value them the relationship cycle can begin.

Relationships can grow a lot of business, but preparation and listening also need to come into play. Building relationships is what makes it happen. We don't grow our business without expanding relationships. You may get a few opportunities, but, for the most part, the money follows the relationship. So, in order to grow your market share, you need relationships. Once again, **please don't confuse relationship building with the relationship type of salespeople.**

We all have some existing relationships. Let's say you have a nice $5 million book of business. And every one of the surgeons that you sell to is using every single product that you have to offer them.

At that point, that $5 million is the ceiling. You can't grow it anymore. Knowing that, if you have a change in your contract pricing, that $5 million drops. Well, when it drops, you lose income, and your competition may even get a foot in the door.

When a doctor leaves your area, there's another drop. So, the only way you're going to get back up to ground zero, which is your $5 million, or expand new business growth, is to develop *new* relationships. This is a very fundamental thing I will talk about throughout this book, but it is the basis of all things—it is indeed the foundation.

How do we build new relationships and maintain the existing ones? How do we take our best customers and leave them alone and develop new relationships with a competitive surgeon across the street who they don't even like? This is most difficult; however, it must be done. A company can't exist unless their salespeople are out building new relationships to generate NEW business. This begins at a very basic level.

Trust

What does it take to build a relationship? The biggest thing it takes is trust. Trust doesn't just happen. First, we have to listen. When you ask the customer a question, the entire encounter is about you being a good listener. If you listen to what he or she is saying, you start to build trust.

Listening

Let's say I'm meeting Dr. Jones for the first time, and I want to talk to him about this new hip fracture product, and I say to him, "Dr. Jones, what is it that you like about the current hip fracture system that you're using?" He says, "I like this feature," or "I like that aspect." At that point, you're prepared to have a conversation about whatever your competing product is.

So, here's our challenge: How do we listen to somebody and truly hear what they are saying?

Active listening is when you stop thinking about what you want to say or respond with, when someone is speaking to you. Once you master this, you will hear and retain more while gaining trust.

Value

The next basic fundamental thing is value. While we're listening, when the customer tells you what's important to him or her, you follow that path. You talk about what's important to them, not necessarily what you want to talk about. You can get back there any time. We want to build trust, because if that person knows you're listening, they know that you value them.

The customer's value is most important—not ours.

When they know you value them, then you get a chance to prove your value; but if they think that you feel you are more important than they are, you're most likely not going to have a chance. You won't get that chance to be in the surgical suite, to show them how great you are. If you're good at what you do, then you need the chance to prove it. Once that happens, you start to build that relationship.

There are a lot of sales reps out there who are really excellent at what they do. The surgeon/customer considers them a part of their team, and that's the goal. That means you become a consultant, not just a box-opener, or an order-taker. To become a consultant—in this business or any business—is where the passion is, and it comes from building trust.

We must get to this point so we can ask the "challenger-type" questions— the ones that take them out of their comfort zones. [2]These questions are at the heart of what your product has to offer. Once you can raise these, you are very close to making the sale.

---

2   Dixon, M., & Adamson, B. (2013b). *The Challenger Sale: Taking Control of the Customer Conversation*. Penguin UK. This work is dedicated to specific methodologies of growing business.

Step One: Preparation

I have facilitated around 150 Master Series classes over the last six years, and one of the questions I often get asked is, "What is your silver bullet?" (this is that one key thing you can ask and get the business.) If there is a silver bullet, it is in your preparation of the information and how you prepare for your presentation. That's your own personal "silver bullet."

Preparation should be completed before the beginning of all appointments or discussions. There are two parts: the topic/product and the customer (in my case, the surgeon). Each of these needs its very own focus. Better, advanced preparation leads to a more efficient, laser-focused conversation that leads to next steps and shows customers that you respect them.

When you meet somebody for the first time, you only have two to three minutes, if you're lucky. It's important you do these things right. It's important that you keep in your mind that you don't get a second chance to make a good first impression. Your silver bullet is how you prepare, and how you utilize that information going forward.

I have always had a passion for teaching, and now, in my most recent role as national director of sales development, I am 100 percent committed to sales development.

This ever-changing world continues to amaze me, and I know we all must strive to adapt to it. However, the foundations of the craft called "sales" are pretty much constant. Basics need to be revisited on a consistent basis, and if we don't, we lose sight of reality, lose market share, and miss out on new growth opportunities.

There is not any athletic team anywhere, whether it be high school, college, Olympic, or professional sports, that doesn't spend a majority of its time practicing the fundamentals of its sport. So, unfortunately, I am compelled to inform you that there is no simple answer to the "silver bullet" when it comes to success. Your willingness to continuously prepare and revisit the fundamentals of your craft is your solution to finding that elusive silver bullet.

The "silver bullet" is what most reps want to know so they can be successful ... that one thing to ask the customer ... unfortunately ... there is no simple answer.

The Product

I'm a real believer in breaking things down and keeping them simple. You can't be effective in two to three minutes unless you're focused. And remember, you're building a relationship. You may have to do what I call "advance the sale." This means multiple trips in front of a customer. Please keep in mind that the more contacts you have, the better relationship opportunities and more potential sales.

I suggest that you work through all of your sales brochures and data and compile it into a reusable presentation folder.. This is where you take your company's literature/ collaterals and choose the ones that don't have too much information on them (too busy).

Select your Literature props from:

- Design Rationales

- Surgical Techniques

- Trade Journal Ads

- Marketing Product Information Slides

- Marketing Sales Education Slides

You want simple clear images of your topic, nothing too busy, in fact, your primary topic piece should be your cover. Only use pieces that support the direction you want to take with your presentation. Please be aware, that you must know everything relative to what is on each piece or peer review paper. I guarantee that you're going to own the information if you take this simple step. And when you own the information, you are showing this new customer that you are prepared. They will pick up on that. You will earn respect through your preparation. Efficiency and respect lead to a lot of good things.

The Customer

After product, the next part of preparation is "the customer." In today's world, finding out about the customer is different than when I started. Today, if you're calling on a new surgeon, you go to their website to find out where they did their residency and fellowship. You get a good idea of their background and what they specialize in. Now you can call an associate who covers the account listed on website, and ask that person if he/she recalls this resident, fellow, or surgeon and also find out what products the potential customer was exposed to during their tenure at said account. A side bonus to this technique is that you have the opportunity to build a new relationship within your company and add to your network.

Part of this preparation should also be what you are going to wear. I realize that most medical sales representatives wear surgical scrubs for their day; some actually wear scrubs from home. While I am not a fan of this, I do understand. I believe that business attire is still the gold standard and if you want to make a difference, here is one opportunity to do so. This way if you have an occasion to unexpectedly meet an upper level administrator in the "C" Suite, you are ready.

Throughout my career, I've met many surgeons who don't know me from Adam. When I meet them, I say, "Yes sir," "No sir." I am not being obsequious, just respectful. This is my style. Your style is your style. Don't change it; make it better. That's all. Just adapt it to the next level and be consistent.

Let me go back in time to a year, maybe 1974, when I took a trip down to Poughkeepsie, New York. There were two hospitals there. I didn't have any business in either of them, let alone the money to pay for the gas to get down there. But I made the trip.

I parked and walked into the main entrance, saw a phone booth in the lobby—you know, the place where Superman changes his clothes. Now, in the phone booth, there was also a phone book. Fortunately for me, the rep who preceded me didn't rip all the Yellow Pages out taking the hospitals and surgeon listings (standard procedure). That's a bad day at the beach.

We had to carry a pocketful of quarters back then. There were no cellphones, no pagers, no computers. I took a quarter and put it into the phone, dialed the hospital's main number, and asked for the page operator. When I got the page operator, I said, "Ma'am, would you please page Dr. Jones for me?"

Shortly thereafter, the page operator came back on the phone and said, "I've got him."

Yes, I was nervous. I'd never met this guy at all. I had to make a sale.

Finally, Dr. Jones came on the phone. I said, "Dr. Jones! Hi, my name is Robin Durni. I'm your new sales representative for company "X". I'd like to introduce myself to you, if possible, today."

He responded, "Sure. Come on up…." Click.

Sometimes doctors hang up on you. That's not a good day at the beach either. It definitely takes the wind out of your sails. But that day, I was in luck.

But, I didn't know exactly what he meant. "Come on up?" Where? I'd never been in this hospital. So, I walked up to the information booth where the little lady with the pinstripe dress sits, and I said to her, "Ma'am, I need some help. I got disconnected from Dr. Jones. He told me to come on up. Do you know where that might be?"

And she said, "Oh, Dr. Jones is an orthopedic surgeon, he would be on the sixth floor. That's the orthopedic floor."

I ran upstairs, and I walked out to the middle of this large lobby. There were two guys in white coats. I thought, *They've got to be doctors.* So, I walked up, extended my hand, "Dr. Jones, how are you, sir?"

He said, "I'm not Jones. That is."

I turned around, and Jones was hauling it down the hallway, his coat flapping in the breeze. He was like 30 feet gone. I thought, *okay, I'll meet this other guy.* He was doing the same thing in the opposite direction—like quail taking off. just going *Poof.*

What did I really need in order to be successful that morning, as far as meeting them? I needed a photograph, didn't I. I needed to know what they looked like. When you Google somebody today, you see their picture. I didn't get any business in that hospital for probably five years. Nothing. Squat.

Bottom line: I don't think I made a very good first impression. But I also wasn't really as prepared as I should have been either. I didn't have the phone numbers ahead of time. So, it was really on me to get better information and be more prepared about who I was looking for.

Remember, there were no computers, web sites or cell phones available at that time. We moved at a snails pace compared to today.

I learned from those opportunities that I had to figure out another way to get through the door. I had to go after business that these people weren't protecting. So I made it a point to know the people in the doctors' offices, and by building those relationships, I eventually got some of their office business. Many customers use non-surgical products in their offices, so there will be someone in charge of the ordering. Take the time to build a relationship with this person. If you can get your products into the office, you will have more exposure to everyone and soon will have more opportunities to have surgeons/customers notice you. This is not an easy task as these individuals already have someone they are comfortable with. The key is to find out what is of value to them and take their service to another level.

One method I used to gain access to the OR was to offer the supervisor my service of sharpening their instruments for no charge if I could set my sharpening stones up on a table in a traffic area so I could meet surgeons as they moved in and out of OR. There were very few disposables at that time so I sharpened osteotomes, curettes, cartilage knives, etc. Shortly after I began this practice my instrument business and staff relationships grew.

Suddenly, the doctors were seeing me more, so then they were more open to talking to me about getting the big stuff. So, don't always go after the homerun. Sometimes it's useful just to get to first base. Remember, relationship building fundamentals are key.

Fast forward to the current time … … …

The distributor for Connecticut is one of my very best friends in life, Bob McEneany. As an independent distributor, Bob was one of those who set the bar for performance excellence and eventually was voted *man of the year* by the Connecticut State Society of Orthopedic Surgeons. That's just how good he is.

So, one night, Bob called me and said, "Robin, can you come down and do a dinner presentation on our new Total Knee and advanced bearing systems for me?"

This was our highly innovative Total Knee System with a proprietary bearing surface. I said, "Yes. How about next week, Monday?"

He said, "That works. I've got a surgeon…" So he told me all the things I'd have to know. I need to know what the surgeon was using, why, how long, what his volume was, his background. Information like that is what I researched before any and every appointment.

I like to know that before I walk in front of a customer. So, Bob gave me all that information, and I prepared for the dinner. Now when I do a presentation at dinner, I bring a small sample kit, and one of my portfolios that I mentioned previously, and on the very front page is what I want to talk about. That way, I can use the portfolio as a prop and have all the backup, if needed, at my fingertips.

So, I met Bob at the restaurant where we would meet this surgeon. Here's the background: He was a big volume *joint guy* in the area and never wanted to use our product because he didn't like the senior rep at the account. Bob hired an associate sales rep solely to meet the other doctors who weren't getting exposed to or educated about our products because they didn't care for the senior rep.

After about a year, this young rep, whose name was Steve, invited the doctor to join us for a dinner meeting. But the way he said it was so cool. He said, "Doctor, I feel bad that I'm not doing my job for you. I think it's my job to educate you about our products so you can make a decision whether you want to use them. Maybe once, twice, or three times a year we could do a dinner meeting, and I'll bring in a guest speaker. Would you be interested in that?"

The doctor said, "Absolutely." Now that's a really nice way to go about building a relationship with somebody who has not had an interest in us.

Over the course of that first year, that's all this rep did—develop a relationship. So, I went to the restaurant with Bob and the rep, and I asked the hostess, "Where are you going to seat the McEneany party?" She showed me on the computer dining room map. I said, "I don't want to sit there. I want to sit back there out of the way.

So, she took me to a round table, which I loved, and I said, "Okay, Bob. Here's what has to happen. The doctor is going sit here at the top of the table."

The doctor brought two of his staff with him. I want the rep that covers them sitting to the doctor's left. I would sit to the doctor's right. I wanted Bob to sit to my right, and I wanted the two other people from the doctor's world sitting to Bob's right. I said, "Bob, your task is to take care of the two staff and entertain them. Steve, we can debrief together after we leave. You know this surgeon the best, so I will need for you to concentrate on his reactions to my presentation." Every dinner I ever host has a plan. It's an event. You can't go in and just sit down.

When everyone arrived, introductions were made, and I began. All I had to do was turn my chair and face this doctor. I introduced myself to him again and said, "I understand you're interested in at least hearing about our new kinematically designed total knee with new advanced bearing system.

I wanted to go through all the steps I always use in a presentation. First, I qualified what he was using and why. I clarified, "I understand that you currently use a fixed bearing and rotating platform."

He said, "I do."

"Well, I'm curious, sir, do you use the rotating platform for most of your knees?"

He said, "No, I do not."

"Do you like it because you cut the proximal tibia in zero degrees, and you can change your rotation center very quickly?"

He said, "No, I just like it because I am comfortable with it. I trained with it."

That told me something right there—that it wasn't all about his competitive rep. I said, "Thank you for that information. Can I start to talk to you about this new system?" I held the brochure up, and I started talking about the femoral component first, which is an anatomically designed component made of our new material for advanced bearing.

This triggered a response from him, and he said, "You know, you guys had a product out a few years ago that did a medial uni-femur combined with a patella femoral all in one with a uni-tibia on the medial side."

I said, "Oh, sir, I think you are referring to system X."

He said, "Yes! I thought it was really cool. I never used one, but I thought it was a great idea."

Now, despite all the noise in the background, I was focused on this surgeon, and I totally changed direction, to go along with his comments and said, "So do you do a lot of unis (Uni-compartmental Knee Arthroplasty) as well?"

He said, "Yes, I do."

"So system X appealed to you because it retained the cruciates and resurfaced the patella femoral joint as well as the medial femoral condyle more so than the uni does, if needed?"

He said, "Absolutely."

"That is important to you?"

He said, "Yes, it is."

"Just a moment," and I picked up my iPad, and found a picture of the prototype of our new tibia base and said, "Does something like this appeal to you?"

And he said, "With that kind of femoral component?"

I said, "Yes." It was a cruciate-retaining as well.

He turned to the rep and said, "I'd like to have that for a case on Friday."

Amazing, had that ever happened to me before? Very seldom. Then I said, "Well, sir, unfortunately the product's not even in LMR (limited market release) yet, but would you be interested in looking at the instruments if possible?"

He said, "Oh, I'd love to."

I replied, "Great! Here's the help I need from you in order to make that happen. If it's at all possible, register for a plant tour and system presentation through Bob." Then I explained the whole thing, and said, "It's best if you travel on a Thursday, come back on a Friday evening."

He turned to Steve and he said, "Work with my office to get dates." Just like that. He was truly interested in something that benefitted his patients. He knew immediately—when doing the uni compartmental knee with more extensive disease than expected, he had to bail out to a total and take the cruciates. He didn't want to have to do that. I was listening to him and that's what drove this presentation bus.

We discussed the next steps. This whole thing didn't take five minutes on my end.

When we got in the car and started to debrief, I opened my little black book to record the debrief steps we were about to discuss and said, "Okay, we've got to get approval for the tour. I'll call our area vice president and bring him up to speed," and then "I'll send the doctor a thank you letter for his time and with the next steps that we're going to do. Bob, would you please get those three dates as soon as possible and send them to corporate so we can lock up the Friday that works best for the doctor."

We had a plan. I went back to the hotel. I always carry FedEx envelopes and air bills with me. I took a piece of hotel stationary, wrote a thank you note to the doctor with the follow-up steps we would take, put it in a FedEx envelope, walked downstairs and put it in the box. This was Monday night. He had it Wednesday after he came in from surgery all day Tuesday.

Bob went to his office and got dates to go to the surgeon's tour. That was the fourth contact. Bob stopped by to visit him again to make sure everything was in line. That was the fifth contact. The surgeon went to corporate for surgeon tour—oh, you fly together, that's the sixth.

The doctor does the tour, meets all the appropriate people from the company in presentations, cadaver lab, etc. We set it up to have the best people engage with the surgeon. Now we're at seven and eight. So, you see how these contacts can add up?

On the way home that night from his tour, the doctor told the rep he never believed in the advanced bearing metal until he had the presentations during that trip. But he told the rep, "If you guys had that product, X—a total knee that retains both cruciate ligaments, I'd be using it tomorrow."

Here's the dangerous part. We had gotten the surgeon really interested before the product was even available. How would we keep the customer happy? We needed to have a plan for that. We had the head of the knee team, come up and visit him. So, these are the steps we take between debrief and follow-up. Follow-up has to be done quickly. The more contacts, the better.

Consistent, respectful persistency wins the day. Advance the Sale.

What sort of preparation do you use? Whatever it is, it should be done well ahead of your presentation.

I got into the habit of building a presentation portfolio for each product upon release. That combined with the appropriate samples I would be ready to go for whatever in advance, all I had to do was review.

Step Two: Research

As you can see from my meeting with the surgeon about the Total Knee System, hitting a home run with a new client requires research. You've got to find out what's important to the customer. You have to ask the right questions. You have to build the best opening statement. Something that will result in dialogue.

Why is Dr. Jones using whatever product he's using? This could be considered a part of preparation, but I contend it is a different category which takes a separate assignment. This research is about consulting other individuals in the circle, such as Residents, Office Staff, PA, Scrub Tech, Nurses, or Materials Management.

These research questions might include:

- What hip fracture device does Dr. Jones use?
- What hip fracture devices do the hospital keep on the shelf?
- Does the hospital allow new systems to be brought in for evaluations?
- If so what is the protocol?
- How do I find out who is on the Value Analysis Committee?

It is important that these questions do not sound like an interrogation, so this usually gets accomplished over a period of time.

If you make real sales calls, are you in the habit of writing down the questions you want to ask? I would suggest that your chances of success are much greater if you do. If you can write down three or four probing questions that might go in different directions and an objection to each of them, your chances of doing something positive in three to five minutes are much greater.

Remember to begin your questions with Who, What, When, How, and Why. For example, "How does device X give you the results that you desire?"

We want to find out what's important to the customer. When he or she tells you, hopefully you are "actively listening," and then you talk about that. You don't start talking about something else. Talk about what is important to the customer. You can always circle back to get to what you were prepared for another time. This is key to building trust.

Results, efficiency, track record, publications, and patient satisfaction are only a few of areas for discussion.

Many times I would ask Operating Room staff about Dr. Jones and what he liked about "product X." One time a technician informed me that Dr. Jones was struggling with a specific adjustable angle guide. I crafted my initial presentation to mention our "new angle guide" and how user friendly it was. I did this without revealing I had been given information by the technician. The doctor gave me an evaluation based on that three minute talk, as my next move was to set up appointment to show key new instruments including our new angle guide.

Remember, when researching needs by having discussions with staff, do not make your research seem like an interrogation. This information can be truly useful to you, and you need to show as much sincere respect for these people as you do to the doctors.

Probing Questions

Most sales representatives are NOT in the habit of writing probing questions down. You really need to practice this as it is an art. "Winging it" is not an option if you want to be successful.

Imagine you're a sales rep going in to speak with a surgeon. You haven't done your research, you haven't done your homework, and you try to wing it during your initial discussion. The meeting starts to go badly and you have no way of getting it back on track. You know how a dog can sense fear in you when you start walking up to them? They can sense fear—they can tell. Surgeons can tell too. They can sense that you don't have your act together. And if they sense it, where they're going to take the meeting all depends on what kind of mood they're in. You don't want to leave your sales and your relationships to chance. The only other option is to prepare.

Let's give it a try... ... ...

Write down the four words WHAT, WHO, WHEN, HOW.

Write down one probing question, using any one of these four words. It's got to start with one of these four words. "Dr. Jones, I understand that you've been doing this, and this, and this. What is it that you like about that? How do you do this?"

Be careful about asking a prospect what they dislike about something. If you're building a new relationship, are they going to tell you the things they don't like about something? Most likely not; they're going to defend what they're using. They're going to tell you they're doing great.

Therefore, I like questions that get them talking about their experience. There are a lot of salespeople who say, "Well, it's not good to talk about what somebody likes about something, because then they focus on the positive." Well, guess what? He's been using it for 15 years. If he was having bad results, don't you think he'd have changed by now? Ask the surgeon what he does like to open up the conversation and build rapport. Then move towards deeper questions, like "Why".

By starting the probing question with the word why, you can dig deeper into the response. This is when you can launch into the real reasons behind their decisions and insert other possibilities and the ease of transitioning to your product.

Please note, write your probing questions down in your debrief / scheduling book. This way when you do a personal debrief you can make note as to what you used and did it work.

Why ???

Let's talk about one of the key starting words for the probing questions. To dig deeper, use the word "WHY"

Why do you believe in this product?

Why did this product get developed?

Why do customers use this product?

I incorporate the word "why" in marketing messages to provoke thought and questions from a customer in my opening dialogue.

I know I mentioned this before, yet it is worth repeating, most sales are made through emotion (benefits), rather than through logic (features).

Oftentimes, we're talking about features all day long. When we describe our new kinematically designed Total Knee, we talk about how it replicates the Normal knee. It has an anatomically designed proximal tibia, medial and lateral, and an anatomically designed femoral component that helps recreate normal kinematics, throughout your range of motion, while helping to minimize mid-flexion instability. Who else can scientifically offer that? Nobody. But are we owning the market? No.

So, what's going on? Maybe we're going about it the wrong way. We spew out features and we're **not** talking about why this benefits the patient. I'm just offering you another way to think about your mission. Don't throw your features away, but think about the mission. *Why* did we design such a system?

You can say a lot with less. You don't need a lot of words. Don't ever put yourself in a corner. Use "WHY" in your product messaging.

So, then there are objections. When you build a probing question, in your mind, you know the surgeon may come back with something. Objections are so important! They open the door for dialogue. There's an 800-pound gorilla in the room no matter where you are. Get it out. Deal with it, and you'll win quicker. I'm serious. You'll win quicker.

Step Three: Listening

Not listening effectively is potentially our most common mistake. While many of us think we are good listeners, we do in fact miss the boat. We are not truly listening until we can focus completely on the customer while a customer is speaking.

Many people act like they are listening, but they are thinking of what to say next while another person is talking. We must clear our mind so that we actually hear what is being said. Then we can respond properly, and show respect.

How do you ask a question, stop thinking about everything else, and listen to the customer's response?

You look directly at the person without allowing your eyes or mind to wander and prepare to repeat back what the person is saying. In order to repeat it back, you have to understand and retain it. If you don't understand a certain point, ask a clarifying question. This is called active listening.

Active Listening means listening to what someone is saying without thinking about what you want to say while they are still talking.

The whole key to making "building trust" a victory is listening to what was just said. If you're thinking about what you want to say next, you're not hearing what the customer just said. How often have you met three or four people at the same time? How often did you not remember all of their names? It happens every day. Retaining names can be difficult. You meet the person, you shake their hand, and then you go to the second person, you shake their hand, you get to the end of the line, and you've already forgotten the first two names.

A technique I have learned is, I clear my head, shake their hand, look them in the eyes and I repeat each person's name before I move to the next one. This helps the name stick a little bit better. This takes practice but it is worth it.

The three components to active listening are:

- Clearing your mind of other thoughts
- Focusing on the eyes or mouth of the person who is speaking
- Repeating back what you hear the client saying every once in a while to confirm you are receiving what has been said

Once again, active listening is key to showing respect and building trust.

Listening shows people that you value them. I can't tell you how powerful that is.

[3]The following five tips are spot on! They apply not only to business but also should be utilized in life in general.

5 tips to start listening before a sales call begins

1. Clear your mind of distractions so you can focus 100% on the customer - make notes or tasks lists that you can pick up later.
2. Pre-call plan so the sales calls is focused and you prevent brain freeze.
3. Plan in advance to limit the time you spend talking to 20% to 25% of the conversation.
4. Drop the assumption that you already know exactly what the customer needs or will say.
5. Turn off your tablet, computer, phone and other beeping devices.

---

3   Spirer, J. (n.d.). 5 Tips to start listening before a sales call begins. *Sales Momentum*.

Step Four: Body Language

Body language is a form of nonverbal communication. This is where a customer tells you something without saying a single word. They indicate some sort of response—non-verbally—to what you are saying. It is imperative that you maintain eye contact during these crucial moments.

[4]It would appear that over **half** of all communication is body language (Mehrabian & Wiener, 1967 and Mehrabian & Ferris, 1967). It took me a long time to figure out just how powerful that is. For example, my daughter has a whole series of eye rolls, and when she gives them to me, I know I'm in deep trouble. Without her saying a word.

For many years, body language played a role in my life, but I really didn't identify clearly with exactly why until I started in this career in 1972.

When I worked in the steel plant, there were many interactions with different positions of laborers and supervisors. I had to develop relationships with all of them, and a big tell-tale sign that you weren't taken seriously was a lack of eye contact, or even worse someone walking away before you were finished talking. Neither of these are good signs and you should

---

4   Mehrabian, A., & Ferris, S. V. (1967). Inference of attitudes from nonverbal communication in two channels. *Journal of Consulting Psychology, 31*(3), 248–252. https://doi.org/10.1037/h0024648

take action and change your approach with such individuals quickly or people may build their own negativity towards you.

Then came the Marine Corps and Vietnam. Body language is powerful in the military, however, once again I wasn't really aware of it until I reviewed many of my experiences years later. The world of combat doesn't give much time for giving thought to whether you offended a person. Things happen way to fast. Yet after the dust has settled, there is time for damage control if you think you may have offended someone. In the field, there is not much room for personal differences. They will surface when you are in a rear area. One thing for certain, if you are having a face-to-face discussion and the person's face tightens, fists clench, and they take a step toward you, closing the gap, **"stand by!!"**

In terms of sales meetings- presentations, when you're meeting somebody new, are they going to tell you all the ins and outs of everything they're doing? Absolutely not.

What you're looking for is some sort of body language telling you that you just said something of interest during your presentation. It's very important. You've got two to three minutes. That prospective client is not going to give you anything, but if you're detailing something from a piece of literature or a sample, you want to be able to watch his or her eyes.

Here's what happens. Let's say you're the new resident physician in town, and I'm showing you some data from a research study. I put the literature on the table in front of you and want to read it with you and talk to you about it. Now, is the doctor looking at my eyes or am I looking at his or her eyes? No, there is no eye contact because we are both looking down, it is very difficult to read any body language when you are not looking into their eyes.

If I'm presenting to someone, I will hold the piece of literature level with my left shoulder facing the customer so that I can watch them while I talk to them. "Doctor, this new 2.0 brochure is a compendium of papers that we put together for a meta-analysis. And as you can see down here, we have four categories."

The key is watching your customer. So that's very, very important to me. Their body language shows me that there's something going on that I can circle back to. Everybody displays body language of some sort. How someone's sitting at their desk:

Engaged – leaning forward

Neutral – vertical

Laid back, passive – reclined

These are things I look for, especially with people who I don't have a relationship with because they're not going to tell me anything. Over half of all communication is a large amount of information you can gather without a person speaking.

Consider this, you are entering a first time presentation with a new potential customer. You have done your preparation and research. You have heard through your research that this person will give you three to five minutes on an initial presentation. You start knowing that you don't have a great deal of time and that you need to begin the relationship building process in order to get a follow up opportunity. Right away, you notice the customer is not making eye contact and is laid back at their desk. You have two options, one, continue on your way, burn your time, and most likely you won't get that follow up appointment, or two, change tack immediately and get this customer engaged. Try asking them a question beginning with What, Who, When or How. Once you ask your question (that hopefully you have prepared in advance), stop talking, pause, and give this person time to respond. I call this, "letting them get on the presentation bus".

Without an understanding of body language, you may be losing clients on the very first meeting. And these lost clients are the ones who may have been easiest to get on board if you only read their unconscious signals and responded appropriately.

Step Five: Voice Control

Your voice, tone, pitch, and pause all play an important role in your efforts to build or maintain your relationships. Together, these are called voice control. When presenting, it is so important to allow the customer a respectful amount of time to digest what you have said and to enter the conversation. (Let them get on the presentation bus).

[[Pitch: in speech, the relative highness or lowness of a tone as perceived by the ear.]]

Voice control is one of my very favorite things to work on in my presentations. Tone of Voice is 38 percent of all communication. Yikes. Body language, 55 percent, Tone of Voice, 38 percent. Whoa. Do the math. Add those two up. Wow: Only 7 percent of communication is words (Mehrabian & Wiener, 1967 and Mehrabian & Ferris, 1967). All this other stuff is basically non-direct / non verbal communication. This is why **Eye Contact** (pg.34 & 41) and "**the Salesmen's Pause**" (pg.35 & 39) are so essential.

Pitch

In a longer presentation, a change of pitch and tone can be beneficial. You're trying to emphasize a certain point versus another, to make that clear. You can pause before a certain point if you want to focus on something else. Enhance your pitch to emphasize something you want to bring focus on. If you're in a noisy place, you can't talk louder because all you do is contribute to the noise. Instead, talk a little softer to bring the customer in a little bit closer.

Example: When at the AAOS (American Academy of Orthopedic Surgeons), working in the corporate booth which can be teaming with Customers, Marketing representatives, Sales representatives and corporate officers can make individual conversations most difficult. I would move away from the back of table to the front and stand next to the customer- with my back to the table so I could manage control of what I wanted to discuss while lowering my tone and customer would naturally lean a little closer (but not too close as we don't want to violate their space).

There are all kinds of things with voice control that make a difference. Voice control is huge, and within voice control is one of my favorite things that it took me many years to figure out…

Pause

Do sales reps feel comfortable when it's silent? Most of us don't. Most of us keep talking when it's silent because we're nervous; we want to fill that void. However, your customers need to get in the conversation. If you don't stop talking, how do they join ? Your customers need to digest what you've just told them. If you don't stop talking, when do they start to digest? How do they do it? **How can they get on the presentation bus?**

Here's the trick: Learn to use the pause. I like to call this the "**Salesman's Pause**," which is just a little longer than what is comfortable.

The pause is your secret weapon, if you can master it. This gives the customer the respect that they deserve. What good would a presentation be if you didn't have a chance to learn anything from the customer?

For example, case in point, in the late 1970s, I had the opportunity to do a presentation in front of several orthopedic surgeons, about 40 or 50 miles north of Albany.

I had an opportunity to make a presentation on our very innovative device called the Richards' Compression Hip Screw to all the orthopedic surgeons on staff at the hospital. It was a competitor's hospital, as were all of them, and I came in there very prepared. I had my suit on. I polished my shoes. My shirt was just the way I wanted it. I used my carousel slide projector—you know the ones that go click, click, click, click as the slide goes through the process. And I started my presentation.

I had one hour, and at the 55th minute, I had finished, because I had practiced. I nailed it. I knew that information cold. I thanked them, gathered up my materials and equipment, and left the room. I went down to the cafeteria to get a cup of coffee and do a self-debrief.

So, I took out my debrief book. I was going to write down all the things that I learned from these surgeons, and, guess what: I had nothing to write, because I didn't shut up the entire time. I didn't stop talking. I didn't ask them a single question. A total swing and a miss.

It's the last time I did that—ever. I learned my lesson, and I realized I had to get better. I couldn't let my nervous anxiety keep me from controlling what I was talking about and asking questions. That is when I started to prepare all presentations with some sort of pause. I even put a reminder on a slide—ask "X."

Try experimenting with tone, pitch and pause in front of the mirror as you practice your presentations. Then try them in conversations with your family, and then with colleagues. This is something that takes time to perfect and make it sound natural. But we talk every day. This gives you a lot of opportunity to practice all of these voice control techniques.

Step Six: Use of Props

The most effective way to present a piece of literature or sample within a short amount of time is to use props. This technique is designed to **maintain eye contact at all times.** You can also practice on your eye contact in the mirror, make note of how often you drift, this is when you can miss a sign. Remember, you need to make contact with as many people as possible in the room you are presenting to. This is how you benefit from a customer's body language. Most of the time they reveal something through some sort of motion, tilting of the head or raising eyebrows. Holding props up allows you to see all of these details. But props can also be very effective in helping clients grasp a large amount of information. The use of props creates an efficiency and respect through preparation.

Let's discuss the term "props". First and foremost, a prop is a actual sample of what you are showing, such as a porous coated press fit femoral stem as used in Total Hip Arthroplasty. I would suggest having an acetabular component, and acetabular Liner and a femoral head that matches the acetabular liner and morse taper on your femoral component. Focus on presenting only the Femoral stem or Acetabular construct at one time unless you feel you have more time or surgeon asks to see more. Remember, plan for multiple meetings and stay focused. Next, please use corresponding literature, mainly pieces in trade journal so customer can relate and connect the dots. Warning, ONLY USE simple pictures of items we just spoke of. I highly recommend using the picture prop to get the appointment to show the sample prop. You can carry a portfolio of pictures and have multiple things to present without having the kitchen sink with you. Efficiency matters. Select your Literature props from:

- Design Rationales
- Surgical Techniques
- Trade Journal Ads
- Marketing Product Information Slides
- Marketing Sales Education Slides

If you hold a piece of literature a certain way, you can watch the customer's eyes while presenting. I hold the prop between my eyes and the customer's eyes and position it just at the top of my left shoulder. Yes, this is awkward at first, yet it can become most comfortable and efficient. This needs to be done without you taking your eyes off of the customer's eyes. You do not need to look at sample but point to the area you are referencing. With practice it becomes very natural. Develop a style that works best for you.

But, let's say I'm talking to a surgeon about this prop or sample, and they take it from me because they want to look at it. I stop talking. It's very, very important that you allow the customer the respect that they deserve. They are looking at the prop for a reason. There is a 50 percent chance that they are interested. The other 50 is that they are just humoring you. They want to see if they can derail you. Customers love to do that.

When you want the prop back, simply say, "Oh doctor, I have one more thing I'd like to show you." You ask for it back, and you can start back with your presentation. Too many times I've seen sales representatives in a roleplay hand me the sample before they've said a thing. That leaves them with no control, and what's worse, no efficiency. Your presentation has just been derailed.

Now, you're hard-pressed to have a presentation while the prop or sample is in the doctor's hands. While it's in the doctor's hands, if he or she has concerns or wants to ask about things, they will ask you, and then you answer them. But if you want to detail something, get it out of the way, talk about this product and all the great things it can do while you have possession of it. Don't try to do it when it's in someone else's possession. You should not interrupt them. Give them free range to respond.

If they have the prop in their hands, stop talking, because while they're looking at something. If they're truly interested, they're not always hearing you. Just stop. You're not being rude. You're giving them respect. Once again, it's the hardest thing for a salesperson to do—to be quiet.

Think about the whole package. How you prepare yourself with your materials, how you present yourself, how you've practiced. What you're wearing has a lot to do with things. And I know times have changed, but whatever style you set, dance to the beat of your own drum. Don't be like everybody else. Set your own high standards.

Something else I learned the hard way, when showing or presenting an instrument set or portions of one, please consider placing the items behind you or beside you. This technique of putting yourself between the customer and presentation items allows you to maintain control of your delivery process. This way the customer is not able to derail your efforts, when they have open access to your material they are generally not hearing anything you are saying. This works best when you are placed in a patient exam room. Simply put your wares on the patient table, stand in front of it and wait . Have your literature prop ready to review what got you to this point with customer before you start diving into your presentation.

Step Seven: Ownership

There are two types of ownership: the product and how you prepare and practice to promote the product. Building a compendium of any said product helps develop your ownership of that product. Practice your presentation with many others, Residents, Fellows, Technicians, or Physician Assistants before you meet with the target customer. This helps to give you "ownership" of your presentation.

Product "Ownership" is relevant to building portfolios that include techniques, design rationales, specification data and any peer review papers. Peer Review Papers are papers that are published in trade journals and approved by a panel of peers. These are not to be confused with company "white papers." Then of course studying and practicing your presentation. Remember to build your probing questions.

Another important thing to consider is your ownership relative to honesty with the customer. Do you tell a customer if there is a widget missing for his or her case? Absolutely. You tell them immediately, ***before*** the case starts.

For example, suppose you have a total knee replacement that starts at 7:30. You're checking your implants before they even drape the patient, and you find out that size five, left and right femoral components, are missing. You look on the schedule, you know that this patient is a female. Well, chances are, that patient is going to take a two, three, or four. You tell the surgeon as soon as possible, whether it's an existing or new customer. I've won a lot of business over my years because the competitive rep thought he could get away with it.

When the surgeon has cut for a five and you don't have a widget for a five, that's a "bad day at the beach". You know you don't have product there. So, these are all things about preparation and ownership. Ownership is huge. Tell your customers anything they need to know **before** they start the case.

One morning I was in a Total Knee Surgery and, in a room down the hall, a surgeon was performing total knee arthroplasty using a competitive system. The competitive sales representative was in the room with him. My case was moving right along, and I heard the circulating nurse answer the phone. She then looked in my direction and said that the surgeon down the hall wanted to speak with me. While visually staying engaged with the case I was in, I took the call. Apparently, the surgeon using the competitive system made his cuts and the components needed were not complete. He wanted to know if my size x would fit the competitive size y. To be certain, I opened my system specification book and found the size closest to the specs the surgeon gave me. I told him what I had found and that he would have to modify his cuts a bit and that I had said sizes in the hospital with an extra set of instruments which were ready for another case that was scheduled after two Total Hip cases. I knew there would be time to clean and resterilize whatever was used. I then quickly briefed the surgeon in my case as to what was going on and asked if I could use the set to help out Dr. Jones down the hall. He confirmed it would be no problem as long as I had what he needed for his next total knee arthroplasty. Then, I passed the news on to Dr. Jones. By that time, my case was almost finished, so I picked all implants needed and went down the hall to work with Dr. Jones. Long story short, the competitive sales representative had **not** informed the surgeon that implants were missing prior to the case. I was able to help Dr. Jones resolve the problem with my system, and he was most appreciative. In fact, Dr. Jones switched his business to me on the spot.

This is just one example of many times I was able to grow business because someone did not take ownership and alert the surgeon to the fact that everything was **not** in the room prior to the case starting.

As you can see, ownership means knowing your product inside and out, how it is different from the competition, what your kits include, how your product can serve doctors and patients, and presenting all this in a way that **advances the sale** while creating long term client relationships.

Step Eight: Product Relevance

Product relevance was one of the last ingredients of the selling process that I discovered. I can only imagine how much business that I have lost or missed the opportunity to grow by not realizing the value of this important point. We know that surgeons do not like change. No matter how many features and benefits you have that differentiate your product from the competition's, you must impress upon the customer that there are similarities that help them see a common thread.

For example, our new hip fracture device is the most innovative in the industry. Do I start off by talking with the customer about all the different things we have that their current device doesn't? No.

I tell that doctor all of the ways that it's *similar* to what they currently use, the same approach, the same incision. And now, because I've put the surgeon at ease, he or she is not thinking about all the changes. I want the surgeon to start using my product, get used to my instruments, get used to me being around.

Now if I have researched the situation and the doctor starts talking and admits that he's having an issue with his current device, then I'm going to go right into the differences with my product. But that still comes from good probing questions.

When a surgeon does change, why do they change? What's the main reason they make the change? A benefit to the patient is their main focus. Their creed is to take care of the patient, and they're all about treating pain. It's important for you to understand they don't usually change unless there's a significant benefit to their patient.

Please remember change will have an impact on many other people, such as, OR Staff (RNs and Technicians), Central Sterile (Cleaning and Sterilization), Purchasing (ordering and Inventory Control), just to name a few.

So in summary, it is key to present similarities to what the customer is using and highlight the features and benefits that allow your product to function at least equally to the customer's choice BEFORE you bring the value of your product into play. Now you can discuss efficiencies, results, value to patient, and set up next appointment to present samples and or some key instruments.

Step Nine: Creating Value

We must learn how to convey the respect of our product to the customer by *creating value* for it. This can be done through how you hold the product, how you present a piece of literature or even how well prepared you are.

[[**Features Tell, Benefits Sell.**]]

Remember: **Features tell, benefits sell**. It is so important to understand why. Features are the many special things that incorporate design and material. Benefits are the functionality, efficiencies, and results. So, features tell someone what a product is and benefits express why someone should use the product. Create Value.

When somebody holds something a certain way, they give it value. How you hold something is important. If you pass something, or talk to a surgeon, and you hand something to him or her, remember, they have a way of doing things. Understand what they're doing and why they do it.

I had the luxury of going to our first total hip course many years ago in Cherry Hill, New Jersey. When I went to this course, I couldn't afford a hotel room. I slept in my car, and some Jersey reps let me use their room to shower and change.

So, for three days, I attended this course scared to death, because I didn't know what I was talking about, and even more so, I didn't know what I was hearing.

[5.1]It was the beginning of our Total Hip Program, which was our version of the Charnley System (Sir John Charnley, recognized as the founder of modern hip replacement). Our surgeon developer himself, was there. We had a booth displaying all the instruments and implants, and during the breaks, the attendees, surgeons, nurses and staff would come to the booth.

I soon noticed how one sales representative talking to the nurses and doctors handled things. He would hold a sample up, or an instrument, and he'd hold it in such a fashion that it was respectful. I watched him for three days. I thought, *Wow, what a difference that made and how he talked about things when he presented them.* He would move from person to person gaining eye contact with each while simply rotating his body and holding the object deliberately steady.

It turns out that this person was the distributor out of the Philadelphia area, Mr. Fred Mischler, he was already a legend at that time, and I continued to learn from him and his leadership until he retired.

Some of my top tips for creating value through your props are:

- Use cardstock for presentation pieces
- Put them in sheet protectors keeping it crisp and clean
- Carry the sheets in a black case or pouch
- If using an iPad, ensure the screen is clean and free of scratches
- Use photos or screen shots so the screens don't move
- Offer things to others using both hands
- Hold pages or screens respectfully with both hands

All of these things show the client that you respect your wares.

Have you ever seen a Japanese person present a business card? They make it an event, they use both hands, eye contact and a slight bow. This is an amazing custom as it creates Value and Respect in one fluid effort. So although, when it comes to passing something to a customer, I don't use the bow but I have adopted the rest.

Like anything else, this takes practice.

If you combine these ingredients into your presentation, how you perform your presentation, how you show value, it makes a difference. You can still do it in the same amount of time, with more focus and gaining more from your customer through eye contact while looking for their *body language.*

Please keep in mind that holding a sample or piece of literature in a professional manner takes practice. Regardless of whether it is a sample or a piece of literature, hold it still, preferably with one hand between your eyes and the customer's eyes and point to your topic with the other hand while not taking your eyes off the customers eyes. This should be done at a distance that is not too close to the customer or they may think you are offering it to them and this all needs to be done while maintaining **eye contact**.

Remember, when presenting a prop, It is important to hold it still, we have a tendency to move it around, avoid this tendency as you don't want your customer to be distracted from all of this unnecessary motion.

Think about how you can add value through the props you use and the way you create them with higher end materials and in how you hold or pass them to the client. Each industry is a bit different, but the principle of creating value can be applied to all.

Be creative, consider using a clean, pressed, Black Dinner napkin to wrap your samples in. Lay the wrapped items on a table or desk. Now very slowly and deliberately open up the napkin exposing your clean, polished, pristine samples. They stand out beautifully against the Black Dinner napkin while protecting the customers' furniture. When you complete your presentation, use the same deliberate method to wrap up your samples. This simple effort shows the customer that you value your products.

Step Ten: Advancing the Sale

I believe and teach that the more contacts with a customer, the better, and that you never really close the sale. We can lose business at any time, so therefore, we must continue to advance the product to the customer. Never take your foot off the peddle. Accepting closure can lead to complacency and that can lead to churn.

"Churn" is the loss of business or sales force.

Advancing the sale is a different thought process. Everybody talks about closing, but do you ever stop selling to that customer? I hope not. If they are using your product for five years, two years, ten years, do you ever think that sale is closed and that you don't have to stay on top of the customer? You have to keep educating customers about what's important and new. This is a key to preventing churn.

It's imperative that our initial presentation is planned for two to three minutes, followed by another appointment, two to three minutes, followed by another appointment, two to three minutes, et cetera. Plan for more, just in case, but keep it focused and brief.

And during that time, you're having follow up and other kinds of contact: emails, texts, whatever works for that customer. The more contact, the more chance of the sale, and keeping the business is important. When it comes to key customers, I used to lay awake at night thinking how I could keep them interested and loyal to the products.

What would I do to ensure that they knew I still valued them while I went out and developed a new customer? I'd follow up with them. I would make sure they were happy with both the product and the new rep. You must keep your finger on things. If they don't see or hear from you, they start to think you don't care as much. If they sense you don't care as much, you're in trouble. That can lead us to churn.

What worked for me was to make a formal appointment at their office with them, and I'd show up dressed for the occasion. I showed up prepared to talk about something new related to what they're using, about an advancement or a peer review paper. I'd talk to them about something new the company had. Even though customers aren't necessarily willing to change, I always felt it's up to the surgeon to make that decision. It's not our job to make it for them.

Many sales people choose not to keep their key customers up to date on their company's latest and greatest. I can tell you that your competition sure will.

We lose a lot of business because we hunker down and we don't want to have to do more work for ourselves by educating customers, or bringing in a new product. That means new teaching, new education, new learning curve, for yourself, the customer, and the staff. If you've got a guy that's giving you solid business, you'd better be taking him somewhere—to a corporate tour or a hands-on surgeon-led program every once in a while. This keeps him or her at the leading edge of your technology and their continuing education. That surgeon is going to lead you to more new business as well, with other potential customers. Trust me, other people watch and see how their competition or senior partner has been treated.

Sometimes we are so focused on our mission that we forget we are guests in an office or hospital and that the "welcome mat," truly is a gift. This is the primary reason I developed the concept of Advancing the Sale.

Quality time with your customers is most important and remember; it's the little things that can make a difference.

When the office staff or O.R. staff see a salesperson coming, they generally think, "Oh no, here we go, this person will take our doctor off schedule and we have such a full day booked. I may have to work later than usual, and how am I going to pick my child up from school, or practice." Once these concerned individuals learn that you don't operate in the traditional manner and tie up a customer indefinitely, they will grant you a pass, willingly.

The flip side of not trying to complete the entire presentation in one meeting and breaking it up is twofold, one, less unknown information at one time allows customer to digest it and stay focused on what you are saying rather than thinking about something else, such as their patients backing up and two, you are showing everyone that you value and respect their time. This is a huge trust builder. Keep in mind, more visits, more exposure, the better a customer gets to know you. However, if a customer says "tell me more," then have at it as you have been given the green light.

Many times I have walked into a doctor's office to follow up with something they wanted, and I could see him/her discussing an x-ray with a Patient and Resident or P.A. I would stop well short (30 feet) and observe. The surgeon would spot me and either motion me over, give me a sign to wait, or nothing at all. If it was the latter, I would leave and come back later. This is also about showing respect.

Perhaps this is in part why I had many relationships of 30-40 plus years.

Consistent, respectful persistence wins the day. Advance the sale.

Step Eleven: Debriefing

Debriefing is very important because it allows you to document what just happened. This is a key step as it lays the foundation for a follow-up plan. We must record key points of a presentation or event in order to build upon the experience. Then we list the personnel and materials needed for the next steps and their timeline.

Debriefing with Your Team

It is imperative that you discuss the debrief segment with whomever from your team is a part of any presentation/meeting prior to said meeting. Their primary function is **not** to be involved in the presentation, unless previously agreed upon, however to listen and watch for all customer responses and body language. Then, after the presentation has been completed and you are in a private setting, you discuss all of your observations together.

Debriefing with Yourself

Debriefing on your own is somewhat different but the same result is planned. First and most important is for you to write down 5-10 key points on one or two pages as soon after discussion as possible. This needs to be in a private setting. Using just one page to start, leave several spaces between each key point. Now that you have a reference to work from, you can add more detail to each key point at another time.

Start with points such as:

- What did you learn about the customer personally and professionally?
- Were there any gaps in your presentation?
- Which product would be most useful to them?
- Is there further information you have committed to delivering?
- What are the volume needs of the surgeon and the hospital they work at?
- What is needed to advance the sale?
- How could you have done better?

Since 1984, I've been filling one of these little notebooks each year and placing it my cabinet. It started out just being a calendar that I wrote things in, but it became my system.

Actually, I have several drawers in my filing cabinet filled with debrief books and product portfolios, because I needed to get better. I wanted to be the best at what I did, and I felt that I had enough things against me— no training, no formal education, coming from the steel plant. I didn't have the confidence, so I tried to make up for it with learning, studying, being respectful, appreciation, and service. But I would recommend this to anyone. You can always learn from an experience, and taking time to reflect and record your observations is a key method to learn.

In my little black debrief books, I liked to plan through things. I created a system that works for me to keep things from falling through the cracks.

Debriefing may also lead you to look at very concrete next steps. The next steps should always be to find out what the average selling price [ASP] is at the accounts the customer works at. Find out what their potential volume is. How many sets are going to be needed to take care of them. There's nothing worse than getting a customer that does eight of some procedure a week and having only one instrument set. Make sure that the details coincide with the plan.

What about bringing management into it, educating the pod or team leader and the manager that this could be very positive? That's what debriefing's about—the next steps.

So, it is imperative to follow up as soon as possible. My preferred method is FedEx Envelope as the purple and orange color stands out, it is dependable, and very seldom does someone other than the addressee open it.

Efficiency is key.

If I had an appointment with a new customer and there was information that I made a commitment to get back to him soon (whether I drove one hour or four hours to get to him/her), I would drive home and return the next day to make a hand delivery to that surgeon. This usually had a high return on investment as we must prove our intention is to "make a difference." Please keep in mind that a competitor is already taking good care of this surgeon.

Debriefing with your team and independently helps to ensure that you are prepared for the next steps to advancing the sale and continuing doing business. It also makes sure that you are able to learn from anything that went wrong during your presentation. It is a record that you can go back to in the future to remind you of growth points. But most immediately, it makes sure you have a comprehensive list of next steps so that you and the team complete all that you need to in order to finalize the deal and maintain the relationship.

Debriefing and Personal Growth

What if you discover through your notes that you have consistent gaps in listening and meeting the client's needs for relationship. It might be that you're discovering that you have not explored gaps you might have in your relationship with yourself or your past. In the spring of 2016, I met Dr. Daniel Tobin. Dan and I met socially at Starbucks. He had a remarkably sincere and caring demeanor, and we became closer over time through brief chats at Starbucks. After a couple of years, I shared with Dan that I was still having post-Vietnam health issues, some 45 years after returning home. Dan helpfully suggested that I see someone from the Veterans Affairs System.

That is when I made the trip to nearby Saratoga Springs, New York, for an appointment with Mr. Paul Stote who has dedicated his post military life to helping veterans. Paul diligently went about the process of getting me started with the VA. I thanked him, but Paul then squared up with me and asked one more question: "How are you doing with PTSD?"

My usual response was, "I'm fine, thank you," however I totally changed gears and chose to tell him the truth and said, "I'm not sure." Paul set me up with a vet counselor.

Enter Dr. Amanda LeRoy of the Albany Veterans Center. I saw Amanda regularly for a year, and through her talent and efforts, I was officially diagnosed with PTSD. For so many years, I had swept everything related to Vietnam, my mother's death, and my beloved son's death under the carpet. No more.

I continue to see Amanda frequently. No doubt, she helped save my life. I had been headed down the wrong path and didn't have the answers. Amanda has helped guide me through a very difficult journey, but it's one that has brought me to a better place in my life today.

I would highly recommend that if you are a Veteran and think you need some answers, please get in touch with your local V.A. Vet Center.

I think this is the type of self-exploration that all sales people may eventually have to make, to understand themselves better, to understand relationships better, and to communicate and listen better. So, an honest **debriefing** with yourself, may be what brings you to these areas of self-exploration and growth. Find a quiet place, sit for at least 30 minutes with your notebook, and see what arises. Then follow-up. Follow-up with your client, and follow-up with yourself.

Step Twelve: Following-up

If you are building a relationship, you must **follow-up** as soon as possible at all costs. I prefer a handwritten note outlining a review of what took place and next steps. This expeditious effort shows the customer you respect them, value them, and that you are 100 percent about doing what you say you will do.

[5]There is a saying that more contacts/calls equate to more success, and in my experience, there is reality to this thought process. Almost half of all Sales Representatives make one call and stop—no follow-up. Next, a quarter of all Sales Representatives stop after the second call, that totals almost three quarters of any given sales force that stops after two calls. This equates to approximately 5 percent of the total sales of any given company. No company can survive with that performance.

The general rule is that 80 percent of a given sales force writes 20 percent of that company's business, and 20 percent of that same sales force writes 80 percent of the business. The Sales Representatives that contribute 80 percent of the business make 5 or more contacts.

---

5   Marketing in a Recession: What Do the Studies Really Tell Us? MarketingProfs
     https://www.marketingprofs.com > marketing-in-reces...
     The Strategic Planning Institute, 1982; **McGraw-Hill Research. Laboratory of Advertising Performance Report 5262**, New York: McGraw-Hill, 1986.

Does that mean you should make less contacts or more? Correct, the answer is more. Now, contacts don't necessarily mean a face-to-face appointment. If you saw a doctor one time, and did a follow-up, that's the second contact with that surgeon. He called me and talked to me, that was the third contact.

If the prospect is a competitive user, he or she must have a relationship with the vendor that they buy from, and they may be kind of concerned about taking money off that rep's table, which is not uncommon. Therefore, it's important to circle the wagons, keeping things in front of the prospect, but also going after something that might not affect the current vendor's income as much until you at least get to build more of a value with the prospect. Sometimes it takes three to four years to get somebody to change what they are using, be patient and stay the course.

Here is another important technique: How many times has a surgeon/ customer asked you about a product in the hall? He or she may be sincere but they are headed elsewhere, so you will not get 100 percent of his/ her attention or how many times has someone asked you something and you try to give an answer in 60 seconds or less and you don't have a relationship with them.

It took me a long time to figure this one out. But, honestly, you want to know if the person is really interested or not. Here is how you find out. If you are asked about a product, say, " In order to do this great system justice, I need a bit more time. Can you give me some time at the end of the day or whenever it's convenient for you?" And if they are really interested, you get an appointment. If they are not, you find out, and you're not spinning your wheels.

I made myself stop trying to make the sale in the middle of the hallway, it's an easy trap to fall into, ask for the appointment! Then, follow up to grow the relationship.

This Selling Skills program and the Durni Dozen can be utilized in any business model. Basics and fundamentals are pretty much universal. Use the Durni Dozen to enhance your sellers' ability to improve efficiency and focus while becoming better listeners.

"I BELIEVE THAT EVERY PERSON HAS THE RIGHT TO BE A GREAT LISTENER AND TO BUILD THE FOUNDATIONS OF LIFE'S RELATIONSHIPS, UNLIMITED."

So, there it is ladies and gentlemen, each and every one of you can make a difference. Just remember: Preparation and active listening will take your world to the next level. Thank you, have fun, and good selling.

Why I Wrote this Book

I wanted to share with others a program I developed that has a powerful impact on many who participate in it. It's called "How to Sell" Master Series. By using the fundamentals, I have embraced and outlined, you can create an inexpensive and amazing program for yourself or your team.

Aside from the fact that I have made every mistake imaginable, some more than once, my goal is to help as many people as possible to shorten their learning curve while minimizing their growing pains during their journey to success.

The Durni Dozen is the twelve steps of the sales process as they flow, according to my experiences. Something that helps my Master Series sales training attendees is that I spend time discussing how everyone has their own style. I advise them, "Don't try to be anyone other than yourself." So please use what works for you out of these steps. Practice and prepare with your selection and add more later on if you sense it is appropriate.

There have been several key people in my training career who expressed a desire for me to write this book, starting with Valerie Lipe, the super-talented mobile learning design specialist (now director, global commercial training content development, orthopedics & has since moved to St. Judes) who supported me in so many ways including assisting me with the development of my original "How to Sell" PowerPoint.

Next, Kaleb Sunwall, VP of U.S. sales training (now Senior Vice President, Global Commercial Training and Education), who has unlimited knowledge and skillsets in presenting, learning, and leadership. Kaleb pushed for me to develop metrics to give a value to my Master Series format, and thus the ability to track the sales performance of those who have taken my program versus those who have not.

Intermediate and Master graduates had significantly lower turnover, 36 percent. Ortho Master Series grads focused on selling skills and grew sales 6 percent more than their peers at 2 percent or 3 times more than peers.

I believe that a large part of this impact is due to the passion and awareness that has led me to this point in my life and career. Traveling throughout this great country, I provide people with a way of learning, closer to their home, with a different view on how it can be done. Further, I support my teachings with examples of experiences from my own sales career, which has all helped me to make a difference.

Mr. Peter Golden, an established writer and journalist, has spent a great deal of his valuable time giving me advice and direction. Peter has an amazing wealth of knowledge..

Mrs. Rachel Spensieri (Right Word Communications) was instrumental in helping me gain the correct direction during the beginning stages of this work. She truly helped keep me on track with her experience and guidance.

Lastly, Dr. Daniel Tobin has been a steadfast supporter of my efforts to write this book. His experience with his own writings has helped me significantly.

Also a few more key people who have encouraged me: Scott Holdsworth, the former group director, has moved on to other opportunities, but Scott was a solid supporter and consistently made certain that I was doing well, both personally and professionally; John Ware, the group director and an extremely organized and competent individual who I call "the maestro," has been running the recon hip and knee programs; Kyle Hubbard, who is probably the most focused and patient person I have ever known, and who is tasked with the robotics program (and has since with Recon Hip and Knee as well, S&N Senior Commercial Training Manager, Orthopedics, Americas); and the multi-talented Nic Morrison (from across the pond, S&N Senior Commercial Training Manager, Orthopedics, Americas), who reigns over all things trauma. Krishna Yakkala, who is an amazingly gifted mobile content developer, has helped me in so many ways. Mr. Tim Holbrook, our skills trainer, and very well-read student of learning who has helped me in compiling Supportive Documentation for this work has moved on to a new sales/management opportunity. Mrs. Dawn Russell Pinkney, (S&N Trauma & Extremities Franchise Specialist), amazingly talented, doer of all things with a title Unlimited. These individuals make up a large part of my family when I'm away from home.

Each and every one of us consistently works together to continuously upskill all of our programs. This sort of commitment to excellence is priceless, and I am honored to having been a part of this amazing team.

A Glimpse at the Master Series

My "How to Sell Master Series Program" consists of two key segments. The first is selling skills, which includes the Durni Dozen, presentation skills, and collateral data to reinforce content. The second segment embraces the breakdown of core product information. This information is relative to choices made by business owner/principals.

Every marketing franchise has developed beautiful and informative pieces of literature that represent their products. This is where I break down and simplify core product information while respecting and maintaining franchise messaging. This enables a sales force to enhance their presentation through simplification and boost success.

An Approach to Course Scheduling

When it comes to the Master Series programs, alignment with the franchise (marketing team) is imperative when incorporating any core product.

Usually, by December, I am given the sales training calendar for the upcoming year. Once I log those programs and dates onto a master schedule, I deduce what dates are left available for my programs. Then I reach out to all sales leadership individuals with my course options and date availability. Usually by the end of February, I am booked through to December.

Once a course date and content are agreed upon with a sales manager, I forward a formal agenda.

Attendee Selection

[6]Thought should be given to attendee selection. While all sales representatives can benefit from my Master Series, there should be a specific focus as to where you want to get the most "bang for your buck."

The new hires can always benefit from Selling Skills, but they take the longest to grow share. Your top sellers can turn the Master Series to gold faster, but because of their market share, they won't show much share growth.

The intermediate sales reps will give you the largest percentage growth the fastest.

Educational Techniques

Quizzes—Pre & Post

[7]Each of my classes starts off with a pre-selling skills and a pre-core product knowledge quiz. Upon completion of the program, these same exact quizzes (post-selling skills and post-core product knowledge) are given again. The same test is given because repetition improves the propensity for things to stick.

---

6   Dixon, M., & Adamson, B. (2013b). *The Challenger Sale: Taking Control of the Customer Conversation.* Penguin UK. "Relative Sales Performance". pg.152

7   Brown, P. C., Roediger, H. L., III, & McDaniel, M. A. (2014). *Make It Stick: The Science of Successful Learning.* Harvard University Press. (frequent testing shortly after lesson>better retention pg.42)

Flip Chart Exercise

Next, and this is very important, at the beginning of each class I use a flip chart, write down the number of attendees in the class and then ask each attendee what they want to get out of this course. I write each answer adjacent to their number and take a moment to discuss this information with them. I return to this sheet at the end of class to ensure each attendee's request has been covered.

Throughout the class I utilize several Flip Chart exercises. The size of the class will dictate how many flip charts & stands / stations need to be available, and I will usually have two to four different exercises. Utopia would be two to five attendees per flip chart station.

The key purpose of these exercises is to get attendees up out of their seats, engagement, collaborating with their team mates, presenting to class, and this all aids in RETENTION.

By using the flip chart exercise, one can gage enthusiasm and leadership. This is also a perfect opportunity to initiate a competitive spirit, ie: points toward high score or a prize.

I mix/ shuffle the attendees for each exercise so that one team doesn't dominate the day. If this occurs others will lose interest. This also gives the opportunity for most attendees to have a turn at presenting/ teach back for their team. I try not to allow same person to do all presenting/ teach backs.

Role Plays

We all know that most sales representatives dislike Role Plays. This is in part due to a lack of comfort relative to their lack of actual quality rehearsed presentations. This can only become an advantage if practice becomes consistent.

This exercise can be very uncomfortable for most so it is imperative that care be given to the role play format and longevity. Performing a role play in front of peers is not only difficult but stressful. However it is this practice that makes us all better,

After all, no practice, with no one critiquing, usually results in a suboptimal presentation to a customer /prospect.

When I began this program several years ago, I had the class do individual role plays with me. Their topic to present would be one of the core products covered in the afternoon segment, while utilizing the Selling Skills and Durni Dozen from the morning session. Each role play would be five to seven minutes with peer critique after each. This concept worked well, even though the class had to sit idly by and watch for an hour or hour and a half.

Since then, I have changed the role play format to multiple mini-role plays. This technique allows for less downtime for class, more time to present relevant content, and better confidence-building for attendees, and each mini-presentation is still critiqued by the class.

Keeping in mind that I designed this course as an engaging, interactive program with many opportunities for attendee interaction. We all know that sales people have a competitive DNA, so there needs to be a reward for the most engagement and participation efforts by attendees. Therefore at the beginning of each class, I announce "The Fabulous Vegas Chip Contest" in which the attendee who receives the most chips for participation will be the winner, and I FedEx them a book on selling, this as soon as I return home to set the example of immediate follow-up.

So ladies and gentlemen, there you have it Master Series, The Durni Dozen, Selling Skills, and more.

Please remember that as you nominate the attendees, it's all about their level of preparation that becomes their KEY to the "Silver Bullet."

Thank you!

Special People

It truly goes without saying that life's experiences don't just happen. The road we all travel takes many unpredictable turns.

Speaking only for myself, I would not have made it to this point without the countless amazing friends I have met along the way. These friends, including my Special People list, are my family. They have supported me unconditionally on a consistent basis and were my mentors and teachers.

The overwhelming emotion that I experience when I am in the company of these outstanding friends is enough to make one wish that all of this would last forever … their support has led me through my life's work. Many of these special people are no longer with us, however, their impact on my life was so positive and enormous that I would be so remiss not to include them.

I would like to dedicate this work to these special people, without whom I most likely would have faltered along the way and never would have made it to this wonderful place.

Dr. David Abraham

Mr. Carl Ackerman

Dr. Joseph Aiello

Mr. Lew Bennett

Dr. Andrew Burgess

Mr. Michael Connelly

Dr. John Czajka

Dr. Louis Digiovanni

Mr. & Mrs. Eddie Draudt

Major Robert Driver USMC

Mr. Gavin Gullo Durni

Mr. Howard A. Durni Jr.

Mr. Keith Durni

Ms. Kyle Durni

Mrs. Nadine Walsh Durni

Mrs. Patricia Jane Roberts Durni

Mr. and Mrs. Ted and Jeanne Durni

Mr. and Mrs. Paul and Peggy Durni

Mr. and Mrs. Victor and Doris Durni

Dr. James Elting

Mr. Scott Flora

Mr. Lenny Foffa

Dr. Anthony Guidarelli

Dr. David Halsey

Mr. & Mrs. Howard Henry

Dr. James Howe

Mr. Nick Huban

Dr. Jay Johnson

Dr. Jack LaBudde

Dr. William Lutes

Mr. William Kemp

Dr. Michael Kimball

Mr. Robert McEneany

Mr. Fred Mischler

Dr. Stephen Murphy

Dr. James Nelson

Dr. Stephen Nicknish

Mr. Ronnie Pickard

Mr. Donald Priori

Dr. Brian Quinn

Dr. Jonathan Richman

Dr. David Richards

Dr. Michael Ries

Mr. Wayne Semprini

Mr. Thomas Terry

Mr. Todd Usen

There are many more, yet each of these special people was instrumental in the life lessons that continue to fuel my passion.

**Success: The ability to move from failure
to failure with no loss of enthusiasm.
—Sir Winston Churchill**

Supporting Documentation

Here are several works I recommend that I believe support my thoughts moving forward. This information is from writings that I had never seen prior to my efforts in the development of the Durni Dozen and my Master Series Program.

Voice Inflection:

I recently read this information which I believe reinforces my segment on **voice control** .

Katherine I. Miller, "Compassionate Communication in the Workplace: Exploring Processes of Noticing, Connecting, and Responding," Journal of Applied Communication Research 35, no. 3 (August 2007): 223–45

Hoffeld, David. *The Science of Selling: Proven Strategies to Make Your Pitch, Influence Decisions, and Close the Deal* (p. 65). Penguin Publishing Group. Kindle Edition.

Mirroring Rate of Speech and Body Language:

Hoffeld, David. *The Science of Selling: Proven Strategies to Make Your Pitch, Influence Decisions, and Close the Deal* (p. 65). Penguin Publishing Group. Kindle Edition.

This work by Dr. Abbie Maroño is also an excellent supportive read for my **Body Language** segment.

FORBESINNOVATIONCONSUMER TECH

Why Body Language Is An Important Field Of Study

Answer by Dr. Abbie Maroño, Studied Human Behavior Analysis, on Quora: Oct 27, 2022 **https://www.forbes.com/sites/quora/2022/10/27/why-body-language-is-an-important-field-of-study/?sh=4c0f34a92d50**

Relationship-Building, Trust and Rapport:

Hoffeld, David. *The Science of Selling: Proven Strategies to Make Your Pitch, Influence Decisions, and Close the Deal* (p. 65). Penguin Publishing Group. Kindle Edition.

Create Value:

Hoffeld, David. *The Science of Selling: Proven Strategies to Make Your Pitch, Influence Decisions, and Close the Deal* (p. 225). Penguin Publishing Group. Kindle Edition.

Effective Listening:

The key to effective listening is not to listen more, but to know what you should be listening for and not be thinking of what you want to say while someone is talking.

Greg W. Marshall, Daniel J. Goebel, and William C. Moncrief, "Hiring for Success at the Buyer-Seller Interface," Journal of Business Research 56 (2003): 247–55

Dawn R. Deeter-Schmelz, Daniel J. Goebel, and Karen Norman Kennedy, "What Are the Characteristics of an Effective Sales Manager? An Exploratory Study Comparing Salesperson and Sales Manager Perspectives," Journal of Personal Selling and Sales Management 28 (2008): 7–20

Stephen B. Castleberry and C. David Shepherd, "Effective Interpersonal Listening and Personal Selling," Journal of Personal Selling and Sales Management 13 (1993): 35–49

Rosemary P. Ramsey and Ravipreet S. Sohi, "Listening to Your Customers: The Impact of Perceived Salesperson Listening Behavior on Relational Outcomes," Journal of the Academy of Marketing Science 25 (1997): 127–37.

Hoffeld, David. *The Science of Selling: Proven Strategies to Make Your Pitch, Influence Decisions, and Close the Deal* (p. 65). Penguin Publishing Group. Kindle Edition.

Listening and Empathy:

After reading this work, I was even more convinced that Listening and Empathy are so very important.

Goleman, Daniel. *Working With Emotional Intelligence* (pp. 140-141). Random House Publishing Group. Kindle Edition.

3 TIPS FOR BUILDING

Sales and Empathy:

Bruce K. Pilling and Sevo Eroglu, "An Empirical Examination of the Impact of Salesperson Empathy and Professionalism and Merchandise Salability on Retail Buyers' Evaluations," Journal of Personal Selling and Sales Management, Winter

Goleman, Daniel. *Working With Emotional Intelligence* (p. 317). Random House Publishing Group. Kindle Edition.

Rapport:

This work is very valuable in understanding the importance of rapport building. Rapport-building is key to relationship development .

Goleman, Daniel. *Working With Emotional Intelligence* (pp. 209-210). Random House Publishing Group. Kindle Edition.

Bibliography

[1] Harvard Business Review, https://hbr.org/2006/07/what-makes-a-good-salesman

pg. 5 in Durni Dozen, re: Empathy & Making the Sale.

[2] Dixon, M., & Adamson, B. (2013b). *The Challenger Sale: Taking Control of the Customer Conversation*. Penguin UK. This work is dedicated to specific methodologies of growing business.

pg. 59 & 66 in *Challenger Sale*, pg. 10 in Durni Dozen

[3] Spirer, J. (n.d.). 5 Tips to start listening before a sales call begins. Sales Momentum. Sound Advice. pg. 31 in Durni Dozen

[4] Mehrabian, A., & Ferris, S. V. (1967). Inference of attitudes from non-verbal communication in two channels. *Journal of Consulting Psychology, 31*(3), 248–252. https://doi.org/10.1037/h0024648

pg. 33 in Durni Dozen

[5] Marketing in a Recession: What Do the Studies Really Tell Us?

MarketingProfs

https://www.marketingprofs.com > marketing-in-reces...

The Strategic Planning Institute, 1982; **McGraw-Hill Research. Laboratory of Advertising Performance Report 5262**, New York: McGraw-Hill, 1986.

pg. 65 in Durni Dozen

[5.1] sir john charnley total hip replacement - Google Search. (n.d.). https://www.google.com/search?q=sir+john+charnley+total+hip+repl acement&oq=Sir+john+charnley&aqs=chrome.2.69i59j0i512l4j0i22i3 0l3.30260j0j7&sourceid=chrome&ie=UTF-8

pg. 52 in Durni Dozen

[6] Dixon, M., & Adamson, B. (2013b). *The Challenger Sale: Taking Control of the Customer Conversation*. Penguin UK. "Relative Sales Performance". pg. 152

Durni Dozen pg. 74

[7] Brown, P. C., Roediger, H. L., III, & McDaniel, M. A. (2014). *Make It Stick: The Science of Successful Learning*. Harvard University Press. (frequent testing shortly after lesson>better retention pg. 42) pg. 74 in Durni Dozen

www.ingramcontent.com/pod-product-compliance
Lightning Source LLC
Chambersburg PA
CBHW040952170526
45159CB00013B/3114